T0156614

Joie de vivre

Ann Patton

BALBOA.PRESS

A DIVISION OF HAY HOUSE

Balboa Press books may be ordered through booksellers or by contacting:

Balboa Press
A Division of Hay House
1663 Liberty Drive
Bloomington, IN 47403
www.balboapress.com
844-682-1282

Because of the dynamic nature of the Internet, any web addresses or links contained in this book may have changed since publication and may no longer be valid. The views expressed in this work are solely those of the author and do not necessarily reflect the views of the publisher, and the publisher hereby disclaims any responsibility for them.

The author of this book does not dispense medical advice or prescribe the use of any technique as a form of treatment for physical, emotional, or medical problems without the advice of a physician, either directly or indirectly. The intent of the author is only to offer information of a general nature to help you in your quest for emotional and spiritual well-being. In the event you use any of the information in this book for yourself, which is your constitutional right, the author and the publisher assume no responsibility for your actions.

Any people depicted in stock imagery provided by Getty Images are models, and such images are being used for illustrative purposes only. Certain stock imagery © Getty Images.

Print information available on the last page.

ISBN: 978-1-9822-5643-2 (sc)
ISBN: 978-1-9822-5641-8 (e)

Library of Congress Control Number: 2020916467

Balboa Press rev. date: 10/27/2020

ACKNOWLEDGEMENTS

I dedicate my book "Joie de Vivre" to my two daughters, their partners and their children, my grandchildren. They are: my daughter Alyson and her partner Dan; my daughter Jennifer and her partner Louis; and my grandchildren Brennan, Meaghan, and Veronica as well as Emma, Simon and Olivia. They have supported and encouraged me all the way!

Meaghan and Veronica are growing, learning and accepting whatever comes along. They help me to move forward. Being surrounded by their positive attitude makes me stronger! Thank you.

When Brennan was 17 years old, he encouraged me to write a book rather than only helping individuals face to face, one at a time. Brennan, you inspired me when you said, "Not everyone has the courage to discuss their dilemmas with another person, face to face. But they sure would buy this book!" Thank you, Brennan.

Jennifer continuously supports me, without ceasing. I am full of love and admiration for her! Thank you so much, Jennifer.

I also dedicate "Joie de Vivre" to my best friend in the world, my brother David, who always gives me his full support and makes sure I am okay.

I am grateful for the support of my cousins – in particular, Phil and his partner Kelly, for keeping me up there, as well as Matthew, who is so caring and wants only the best for me.

I am blessed by my magnificent friends, Paul Nadeau and his partner Sue. They are both very dear to me. They shared many of their ideas, allowing me to think clearly and be well organized. Paul is a top-notch listener. He had a good ear for my project, and helped me to pursue it smoothly! Thank you, Paul and Sue!

Ann Johnson and her partner Paul Johnson are my wonderful friends. Ann's diligent character, as well her loyalty and selflessness, have encouraged and assisted me in my business projects. She is always there for me. Thank you, Baboush, for supporting me along my path in life.

I am more than happy to include Dr. Fahed Turk, who is my very close friend. I love him dearly and thank him for being there for me!

Last but not least, I thank my editor Mary Trafford, who is an extraordinary person and brought the tools I needed to ensure the contents of my book flow well.

All this is magnificent but it may seem as if I am the star here. I don't want flowers. What I want is for people in need to live with a positive attitude, My hope is that after they absorb and practice the ideas I share in this book, they will be happy and full of energy.

Finally, thank you to all my friends I have not mentioned here – you're in my heart and that's what counts!

Ann Patton
Montréal, Quebec

CONTENTS

INTRODUCTION

The main reason I have written this book, "Joie de Vivre," is to reach as many people as possible, including you, the reader! I want you to benefit from the <u>real</u> riches in life – getting up in the morning with a smile or a good feeling, despite the hurdles and clouds that may come your way every day.

You can succeed once you know how. For example, students who want to earn scholarships know they must get the required marks. This is what "Joie de Vivre" is all about – not only knowing what you want, but also knowing how to get there.

Donning positive armour – a protective aura that cannot be penetrated – along with a sense of excitement is what I call joie de vivre. It's the key to success. Life's roller-coaster ride can be challenging. Having a positive attitude can provide you with a compass to navigate the obstacles and avoid the pitfalls. A positive attitude can become "second nature."

My positive energy translates into a passion and an eagerness to share with others. I witness the change when one moves from being bogged down by stress, negative thoughts and anguish, to allowing space for a life full of energy, peace and enrichment.

In "Joie de Vivre," I offer tools to enhance your life each day with a "second-nature" attitude. "Joie de Vivre" also includes examples of situations that can help you identify with and understand the life experiences of others.

You can decide to organize your thoughts around a positive centre, leaving behind guilt, sorrow, doubt and fear. You can choose to attract what is good for you and become the master of your own "positive" energy, space and control.

Ann Patton
Montréal, Quebec

CHAPTER 1

Our World within the Universe

O ur world is part of the universe. Light and heat from the sun. The sun is a star that emits light and heat, which nourish the earth and allow us to survive on this planet. We human beings can best benefit from and use this positive energy when we live fully, as opposed to simply existing.

We can accomplish positive change by examining the logic of universal rules – that is, by seeking examples of how we humans can live according to our own nature, and adapt to different situations.

Please read the one-page preparation guide of this book before applying the techniques for developing an abundantly positive attitude. In this way, it will feel like second nature to you.

Everything exists in duality. *Polarity* is a "Universal Rule." This means positive energy and negative energy are two extremes on the same pole, each at varying degrees. This concept is similar to other polarities, such as heat and cold, or love and hate.

For example, personalities can have the same effect. A flamboyant person is often outgoing, talkative and vibrant, yet he or she can also be poised, calm, quiet, and reserved, depending on the situation. Consider someone who is with close friends in a low key setting, feeling comfortable and "at home." This same person might be exuberant in another setting.

But when he or she feels at ease, they may be more reserved, and better able to listen and take part in a stimulating conversation.

We often hear that "opposites attract" in reference to people who are able to express themselves inwardly and outwardly, depending on the circumstances. Two individuals in a compatible couple may seem to be opposite in personalities, yet they can get along so well! Having two sides to a personality can be fitting, even desirable. In other words, it's the best of both worlds.

Heat and cold are also examples of two opposites. Consider a person who is used to living in the south, where the weather is often very hot. If that person arrives in a city like Montréal, Quebec, in late August, for example, they may not be comfortable, perhaps finding the temperature too cool. Over time, however, this person will adapt, and grow used to the climate in Montréal.

Heat and cold are on the same pole. Our body can adjust and eventually feel comfortable. The same applies to people who travel in June to a beach in Maine, on the U.S. east coast. At first, they will find the ocean water to be very cold. But if they stay immersed long enough, they will eventually grow used to it. The opposite reaction becomes very tolerable and acceptable.

In a situation of polarity, when we're on the negative side of the pole, we can also try to be on the positive side – that is, we can transform our negativity to a positive approach!

We can adjust polarity on the same pole. We simply decide where we want to be!

However, in absolutes, such as true and false, there is either truth or falsehood, not both. We cannot be less true or more false. In other words, either our statement is true or it is false!

We're lucky that our system can adjust to the dual positions on the same pole, from negative to positive, heat and cold, opened to closed personalities, and so on. Rhythm, which is the universal rule, is never-ending and is in constant movement. For example, waves from the ocean come and go because the gravitational forces of the moon and sun control them. Those forces pull the ocean water upward, creating the ebb and flow of the tides. They also cause the waves to roll onto and away from the shores.

Similarly, situations change constantly and for different reasons – for example, good and bad times in history that may go on for centuries, such as the fall of the Roman Empire or other civilizations. The pendulum swings back and forth, regardless of the situation. Whether it's a failure or a success in business, the rhythmic sway from negativity to positivity is endless. That being said, negative situations allow room for growth, capitalizing on ideas for success.

Rhythm is an aspect of our own experience of the ups and downs of life, which we may find unfair or puzzling. Life is rhythm. When we persist, choosing to embrace the positive side of the pole, we can learn to accept life's rhythm more easily, learning how to cope with the bad times and welcome the good times. As a result, once the habit of positivity sets in, and our strength becomes second nature.

The different rhythms that come and go are part of life. They give us opportunities to endure the bad times. They strengthen our capacity to change from negative to positive modes of living, as opposed to simply existing!

Universal Rule – Cause and Effect

In other words, every cause has a negative or positive effect. For example, a student has an early-morning exam. She sets the alarm clock accordingly. When she attends the exam, she ends up with a positive effect. But if she does not get to the exam on time, the result is a negative effect, which would likely cause her to experience bad feelings, guilt, stress and a loss of focus.

Here's another example of cause and effect. A young man is about to take his driving test, but he hasn't taken the time to learn all the rules he needs to know to safely operate a motor vehicle. This would be the cause. The negative effect would be that he would not earn the legal right to drive a car – in other words, he would fail his driver's test. If his training session is planned in an office environment and the coach is very late (this would be the cause), the negative effect will affect the trainer and the licence bureau employees, whose schedules would be disrupted.

It is important is to understand that everyone is in charge of themselves. The individual person causes the negative effect. The outcome of a negative effect can be overwhelming. Furthermore, negativity inhibits our growth and creates a defeated feeling in us. When negativity engulfs us, our life doesn't go smoothly. We have to get back on track and continue our journey, staying on the path of positive attitude, free from added stress.

Cause-and-effect is a rule that implies choices, the ability to maintain control of our life, and the awareness that good outcomes are possible. As a result, living with a positive attitude can give us a heaven-on-earth feeling!

The universal rules and examples of situations can help you achieve your goal of living on the positive-attitude side of polarity. This way of life gives you purpose and allows you to feel good, from the moment you wake up from a good sleep.

PREPARATION GUIDE

This preparation guide helps you to connect with and prepare for a positive-attitude approach to life, which is presented in chapter two, under the heading "How to Achieve Your Goals."

It takes preparation and practice for you to be able to run two miles without anguish! The same applies to the challenge of changing to positive living, and growing and getting into the habit of a no-stress, on-top-of-things, in-control attitude.

It takes time to learn to live with a positive attitude and to feel as if it's second nature to you. That's what this book is all about – getting on the positive side of the pole and staying there. As acrobats work toward balancing high above the ground, practice is the only way they can achieve that. No fear, no anxiety, nor any other negativity can exist if they are to accomplish such feats. The acrobat must practice until it becomes effortless – until it feels like second nature.

Eventually, you will have a "big-deal" attitude when you are up against a bad situation. You will feel well prepared to take up the challenges. Being well prepared is the key to getting through the rough tides. A surfer gets up, falls and then gets right up again. Practice allows you to have that kind of strength and positivity, and an "I-can-do-it" attitude.

Prepare well, and get your mind ready to get in gear. Like a coin, where one side is negative and the other is positive, you can instantly turn it over to the positive side.

CHAPTER 2

How to Achieve

Whether you're tackling the simplest tasks or the most challenging, to achieve anything, you must undergo a change in attitude. You must accept that you exist on the negative side of the pole. You must be willing to reach the positive side of the pole.

Having a change in attitude is how you can learn to live with positive energy. As I explained in chapter one, the cause-and-effect rule tells us that when we accept a negative effect, we can cope with it – such as when we have made a poor choice. After all, we are responsible for that choice. Facing it gives us the opportunity to create change by making good choices in the future. In turn, this allows us to live more fully.

In other words, when we live with a positive attitude, we'll have a positive outcome. We want this to become a habit! Only <u>you</u> can change from a position of negative energy to one of positive energy.

Let me introduce the groundwork you'll need. The groundwork and your frame of mind must be on the same page of the proverbial hymn book. They must work together, in harmony, to transform a negative attitude into a positive attitude. This is your first step in seeing the light at the end of the tunnel – a transformation that leads to a life-long, positive way of living.

Changing your thoughts will create positive feelings and good results, as well as opportunities to reflect on your new way of life. Doing the groundwork means working from the bottom up. You'll quickly gain confidence and power-up the engine you need to live a successful life, whatever form that takes.

The key is to move from a new beginning, embracing what you choose, to create a new way to experience, understand and achieve results.

If you wake up feeling negative, it means you're at the bottom of the ladder. Moving up the ladder takes practice. You must tackle simple tasks, step by step, and be satisfied with the results. This helps you continue in the same positive spirit. Once you reach toward positivity, you will grow, like a tree that reaches upward, toward the sun. You will flourish, thriving in the sun as well as in the rain.

Positivity is life – it's a way to harmony, motivation and inner peace. You take each hurdle in stride. You don't want to go back to just existing – that is, living with a negative attitude – because you have experienced the difference being positive can bring.

Take this journey gradually. Reach for your smallest goals and allow yourself to grow as you achieve each objective. Let each step empower you until you feel great, fully alive and wanting more. There are no limits to what you can achieve!

Just one step in the right direction marks the beginning of your journey. It takes planning. You must know where you want to go and what you want to explore. You must be interested in changing, and in gaining the benefits of loving every day of your life.

When you're in a negative mode, you'll have difficulty seeing the difference between negativity and positivity. To discern that difference, you must actually experience the positive end of the pole. Transforming from a negative attitude to a positive attitude can be challenging, but you can do it. Being negative is a habit; that's what makes it so challenging to change.

You're in charge of your own life. If you're not living positively now, you will be after you engage in the day-to-day practice of tending to your own growth. Seeds that are well planted and well cared for grow to allow change and new beginnings.

Doing groundwork means you're in charge of your choices and your practice – for example, having a conversation with another person about your ideas can get you started on the right foot. Expressing your thoughts is empowering. It reflects an attitude of positivity. This confidence forms part of the groundwork you can use to get to the other side of the pole and get a grip on positivity.

What you share with someone is important, not only to you but also to that person. They can consider your ideas, combining your thoughts with their own, and vice versa. Together, you can develop an ideology, expanding it and making it more interesting. Your ideas may intrigue them, and this can boost your ego, making you stronger. There'll be more discussion. It's a dynamic process – a two-way street; a process of debate and generating ideas.

Dialogue also strengthens your confidence. It will lead you in the right direction and you'll fulfil the goals you need to stay on track toward achieving a positive attitude.

Please remember this: you are the cause; there is an effect. In dialogue, the back-and-forth exchange of ideas you share with another person has a positive effect on you. In other words, your action is positive and so, you feel better. You accomplish something of value. You're taking steps that support your positive attitude. It's like putting more wood on a fire. Keep feeding your ego in this way, and your disposition and attitude will generate that same good feeling.

Groundwork also means focusing on what you would love to acquire. Your own choice is usually the best one for you – but you might not know how to attain it. In this book, I will show you how.

So, keep reading and act on what you discover. You'll get there. Taking it one step at a time, you'll see that small goals become bigger goals. Slowly but surely, you'll succeed. Please don't over-reach and try for more when you're not ready. This could break down what you have achieved and discourage you.

To put it in perspective, consider that while not everyone is an extrovert, we all want to have a positive attitude. Introverts want to succeed, too. Some may choose a different path and arrive at the same goal – success.

For example, introverts who are already at the positive pole may find that following a new path toward their goals makes them feel better. A walk in the park may ignite a spark that generates a new project, rich with ideas. This can result in a real sense of achievement: you know you did it your way, without negative thought.

Here's another example. If you're artistic, you may express yourself by painting on canvas. Artistic expression can include splashes of colour, or areas of black, grey and white, depending on what you feel. Other artists may express themselves through music, poetry or dance.

Maintain that positive attitude and work on anything you desire. With practice, your ability in your chosen activity will strengthen and improve. If you are in a negative state at any given moment, you might not feel excited about moving on. But you will yearn and crave positive energy, and in time, it will come to you – and it will come naturally!

It is your world. By living with a positive attitude, your life will be exciting. Remember, small steps; never quit. You will arrive at the positive end of the pole. That's what living a good life is all about!

Giving up means going backward. Going forward means success, more energy, and a smile on your face. Take up a hobby and love it, and things will begin to happen. As long as you engage in movement, you'll go forward.

All this will give you good feedback, because you're in charge of your choices. Step-by-step, you will want more. Each of us has a personality; we work with and within our own particular traits. We don't want to be different. You are the only one who knows what makes you tick. Wishing you were like someone else indicates a negative attitude. You're a special person, in and of yourself. You can be an achiever. Something that is difficult for you will seem easy if you create positivity all around you.

Having choices about what you want to pursue will help you smile, sleep well and be excited each morning. You'll feel enthusiastic, whatever the day brings – rain, sun, snow or grey clouds. You will accept what comes, hurdles and all! Come what may, you will get through it.

Why will you endure? Because you live on the positive end of the pole, from morning to night. Rest your head on your pillow with a smile on your face. Life is simple. Take a walk, breathe, watch the birds and smell the flowers.

Learning to really live and taking action to do so mean you'll be satisfied with your achievements. This allows you to grow.

Don't let one day go by without thinking of your new beginnings. Just thinking is a start! Things will seem easy once you get into the flow of living. After all, ours is a fast-lane life, with new technology to learn and use every day. Parents strive to keep life stable so their children can thrive and succeed. They try to achieve work-life balance, which can be a real challenge in these fast-paced times. People who don't have children also face challenges as they tackle the stresses of daily life.

A positive attitude can protect us and help us to live fully. It is challenging to stay positive but it can become a habit. In fact, when it becomes a habit, you can meet any challenge. Having a positive attitude makes life worth living and makes challenges surmountable.

Positive actions are key to a wonderful life, where you take the hurdles in stride! Take the time you need to get over any bump, and your life will change. You will feel the change and want more. What a transformation! Life can be beautiful. That's the result of positive living.

It is very important to not make excuses about things like bad weather, not getting along with someone, feeling someone has stood in your way or someone was too aggravating. You won't get there by saying, "I feel blah today, so I'll wait until tomorrow." It's easy to blame others as you face reality. <u>You</u> are responsible for the change you make to render your life beautiful.

If you are to achieve anything – to grow and change in the right direction and reach your goals – excuses are unacceptable. We all want to achieve happiness. With practice, you can do that.

Like you, I have been through many challenges. I am neither strong nor weak, but I stayed on the positive side of the pole and built up the armour of positivity. Nothing can get through my armour, no matter what challenges I face. When you put on this armour, you'll have true protection. You have to do the groundwork, and assert, "*Vive la différence!*"

Doing the groundwork is effective practice, and it does become easier. That's encouraging. Once you're on a roll, practicing being positive, you will live with a genuinely affirmative attitude. Why? Because you have established the habit. There are so many examples of people who yearn to be positive and happy, yet they don't know how. The trick is not to become frustrated. Start every day with a positive beginning.

You'll get used to it, adding more goals as your energy level grows. Chase from your mind anything that is negative. It must not get in your way. You must do whatever you can to avoid even one negative thought. You can choose how to chase away negative thoughts. For example, to get rid of a negative thought, you can jump up and down 10 times like an athlete; you can ride a bike, skate or listen to music. You must do whatever it takes to clear away the negative thought. You are the boss and you can do this.

This is your first step in the practice of chasing away the negativity. At first, it's is not easy, but it gets easier as you go along. When you're in a good state of mind, the habit feels natural. For example, if you're used to running three miles each day, you don't think about it. You just do it. That's because you worked toward it and have developed the capacity to do it.

Don't think of it as a chore, but as a new beginning, each day. You can start your day well in any way you want, and end it well, too, because you can handle whatever comes your way.

In short, there should be no thinking, just doing!

It's like a volcano. When it erupts, it's impossible to stop the flow of lava. Similarly, you cannot stop the rush you feel about what you want to accomplish by creating a new beginning through the daily practice of positivity.

To accomplish this, you must achieve success every day. Do you remember when you were a child? After riding a tricycle, you wanted to ride a two-wheeled bicycle. You realized nobody else could do this for you. You had to do it yourself. But how? You learned to do it through practice and more practice. It was practice that allowed you to succeed. And it was your choice!

It was similar when you took lessons in swimming, skiing, horseback riding, driving, sailing – the list goes on. The point is, you are the one who achieved what you achieved. And you did not succeed by wishing you were someone else. From a young age, you had within you the drive to win.

Cherish these memories of childhood, with its vim and vigor. They are good memories because they remind you of times when you felt great. You were positive. You achieved your goals. After all, many people say, "I wish I were a kid again. I wish I had that kind of energy." But it is still within your reach. As you age and grow with that same kind of positivity, you will never again say, "I wish!"

Groundwork is the key to getting where you want to be! Once you are satisfied and ready to move on, in a spirit of growth, you will arrive at a place of change and confidence. You will love life, no matter what circumstances you face. Why? Because you are in the positive mode, which is such a good place to be. Your zest for life will remain strong. Being positive keeps you where you want to be. Life takes on a simplicity that is the key to your happiness. When you're living with inner happiness, you can create anything you wish and sustain your own joy.

You may not have had opportunities to ride a bike, participate in sports, or learn to play the piano. Perhaps you lived in an abusive situation. Such experiences do not have to stop you from making changes today. You can overcome past pain by taking hold of the reins and moving in a different direction. With a positive attitude, you can learn to accept the past, even if the pain was excruciating. Positive living results from a positive attitude, becoming a habit.

Renowned music star Shania Twain is an example of someone who faced great challenges in childhood yet achieved success in life. While growing up, Twain lived in poverty and witnessed domestic violence at home. Music was her passion and it sustained her spirit. By age three, she was singing; by age eight, she was playing guitar; and by age 10, she was writing her own songs, and began performing. When she was 22, just as her music career was taking off, Twain lost her mother and stepfather in a car crash. She chose to postpone her career in order to support her three younger siblings.

In spite of all these challenges, Shania Twain persisted. She succeeded in launching her career, achieving music stardom by age 30. In 2011, she was inducted into the Canadian Music Hall of Fame. Twain believes in "playing it forward." In 2010, she launched the non-profit organization "Shania Kids Can," to give underprivileged children the chance to play music or take lessons their families could not otherwise afford.

Olympian, humanitarian and adventurer Clara Hughes also experienced tough times growing up. During her childhood, she was traumatized by her father's alcoholism, and as a teenager, she herself fell into drinking and drug use. Nevertheless, she achieved great successes in life. She was the first Olympian to win multiple medals in both the Winter and Summer Olympic Games, competing in speed skating and cycling. She became the National Spokesperson for Bell Canada's Mental Health initiative and the "Let's Talk" campaign. By sharing her past struggles with depression, Clara has helped break down the stigma associated with mental illness. She is a classic example of giving back to your community, and achieving your best and most positive life.

The groundwork for making such change is the path you want to follow to be your best self. It's as simple as that. It involves pursuing, winning and living – all of which are goals you can achieve. They will help ensure your future happiness.

At the beginning, it all can seem so difficult, even hopeless. You may lack energy and have a negative attitude. But, one step at a time, you'll gain confidence because you choose to achieve and succeed. Anything can seem difficult when we feel low and lack hope. You can change this; you are in charge of yourself and your own life – nobody else is!

Pursuing your goals every day, practicing what is positive, and carrying out the groundwork are the answers! Those who live partly in a negative mode, or temporarily in a hum-drum state of mind, must choose to think positively and be where they want to be. The energy you need will come, you'll regain your vibrant attitude and then you're off to the races, reaching toward the wonders of life – <u>your</u> wonderful life!

The effort you put into it will bring you inner peace, satisfaction and greater energy. As in any sport, with practice, it becomes second nature. You learn to understand what you need to do and you do it, almost automatically!

If you choose to live and not simply exist, you will get through the challenges and be where you want to be – that is, a peaceful life, full of positive energy and the capacity for growth in any endeavor. This is definitely in the works for you.

This is the beginning of a rewarding journey. You can choose to create change, naturally and without struggle. It's gratifying and you'll have a feeling of accomplishment every day.

You know you're ready to embark on this journey when your decision becomes a necessity, and you feel the need to change. You'll have a strong desire to practice being in the positive mode. You won't feel content just to read about it. You'll be in a totally different space – loving life, overcoming hurdles and being amazed at how you continue to grow. It's all about the choices you make and it's about <u>you</u> being in charge of your life.

Embarking on a new way of life means following the suggestions noted below. It's like a map to your destination. You must be unwavering and diligent. No excuses! Where there is change, there is growth. At times, it may be painful, but you can get through it if you stick with it!

When you wake up each morning, open your eyes and practice positive thoughts. If you wake up with a negative thought – for example, "Oh, it's raining!" – change your attitude and think something positive, such as, "It's raining! Wow! We need the rain! It will help the grass grow."

Here are some other suggestions of positive thoughts for starting your day:

Instead of going without breakfast, I'll have a bite to eat, for a change. And I'll have coffee with it! I love a good cup of coffee to start my day!

I'll take my dog for a good walk. She'll love it and I'll find it invigorating. Plus, it will inspire me with upbeat thoughts as I stay on track toward positivity!

I'll start off my day on the right foot by making my lunch, for a change. It'll be nice to have my lunch all ready, instead of having to line up for food at a deli, a food truck or something.

Practice having a positive attitude; it is pleasing to the mind. This will build a new you and make it easier for you to transform to a good life – a life that's full of wonder.

CHAPTER 3

Negativity & Situations

L iving with negativity is like living with a sense of defeat. For many
people, it becomes a way of life. When you get used to living with
a negative attitude, it can lead you down a never-ending path –
toward a kind of deep-seated, negative existence.

In this chapter, you will read about negative situations. These examples
will help to open your mind to different ways of being – the benefits of
positivity, which can enrich your life!

In this chapter, you'll read about a few individuals who are all in the
same boat – that is, they don't know how to enjoy life! Their names have
been changed and each person's story is presented simply as an example,
not as any particular individual.

Here are examples of how you may be living with negative energy:

- thinking you have to accept your "lot in life";
- feeling a lack of confidence and positive energy, not getting enough
  sleep, and so on; and
- missing out on the benefits of living with good energy – that is,
  the positive attitude mode!

You can probably understand what it's like to live with hopeless
feelings – feeling as if you can never get ahead; experiencing headaches,
anxiety and sleepless nights; and lacking in energy. The following are just

a few examples, but they reflect what can happen when you do not truly live with a positive attitude. They are the opposite of living of a good life, which is within your grasp.

Situation 1 (Life – simply existing)

Let's look at an example of a life in which the individual is simply existing, not living life fully.

> *Jacob doesn't feel excited about life. Instead, he just goes from day to day. He sometimes feels hopeless and thinks, "What's the purpose of living?"*
>
> *When Jacob gets out of bed in the morning, he feels down. He has no energy. He arrives at work without a smile. He fakes his "Good morning!" greetings to colleagues.*
>
> *This has become a way of life for Jacob – day in, day out, month after month, year after year. He aims to just get home at the end of the day. Then, he may do little more than watch the news on television.*
>
> *When Jacob's partner asks him how his day went, he just answers, "Same as yesterday – fine, I guess."*
>
> *From Jacob's perspective, it seems that only bad things happen to him. For example, his father has terminal cancer. Jacob's children don't seem to have a strong connection with him, although they all get along well together. Jacob feels he is boring. He is not surprised by how his children interact with him. The way he feels and lives his life tend to impair any possibility for good communications. This shows that when you feel so negative about yourself, your relationships may also be negatively affected.*

Jacob may look forward to a good meal, like a dog, for whom food is a thrill in life. But he just fills the emptiness of everyday life. He watches television, just to pass the time, or eats comfort food, which is only satisfying for the moment. He lives in his own world.

There's not much going on in Jacob's heart or mind. He is submissive to his partner. Sometimes, he wishes things were different. He feels a kind of envy for the lives of others, and sometimes wishes he was someone else.

Nevertheless, Jacob recognizes things could be worse — for example, his partner could leave him, or he could lose his job or become very ill. He continues to feel boring and lacking in energy — and these are only a few of the possible effects Jacob experiences from living with negativity.

Comments on situation 1:

Note that every word coming out of Jacob's mouth is negative, which results in him having no positive energy. He feels as if he is in prison, stuck in a rut, with no hope of change.

Yet Jacob notices others seem to be excited about life. This is a window through which he can envision change – good change! He can imagine living fully, and not simply existing.

Jacob may wonder about other people who smile and have energy. He may think, "Why do they have such positive energy?"

The answer is this: living with positivity would allow him to experience the positive side of the pole, where energy resides. We can all live like that, too. Everyone wants and needs more positive energy! Once we realize that, there is no going back.

And here's the icing on the cake: in life, negative situations will continue to come up, and you <u>can</u> handle them. Once the storm is over, you can move on! That spells success. You have won. You will never return to a hum-drum way of life, such as the life Jacob is living. You will truly live instead of simply existing.

Living your life fully takes hard work. But it's worth every bit of effort. Experiencing life's challenges and living fully continue "till death do us part."

Situation 2 (The humdrum of life)

Let's look at an example of a humdrum life.

> *All her life, Kate has lived with parents who are negative. To her, this is normal, and the results are: she doesn't have any dreams; she has no sense of satisfaction; she has no energy; and she lacks confidence.*
>
> *Kate's family criticizes her every move. Her parents can't understand why she has a hard time getting out of bed in the morning, or why she lacks the motivation to do much of anything.*
>
> *At school, Kate is not interested in any particular subject, including gym, because she has no energy. As a result, she fails to succeed and she lives with a self-pitying, "Why me?" attitude.*
>
> *Kate's friends are similar; each just has a different version of the same story.*
>
> *Kate writes in her diary. It helps to relieve some of her pain. She feels it is pointless to talk to her parents or friends because their responses would be negative.*

For Kate, growing up without ambition feels normal. She thinks life is boring. She regrets being born into such a humdrum life. She has headaches and anxiety. She keeps everything to herself. Sometimes, she thinks perhaps she might meet someone who has a better life than she has — someone who could help her change her negativity, even though she has lived with it since childhood.

Kate wonders why some people actually laugh and enjoy life, without the hang-ups she lives with every day. To make herself feel better, she thinks, "Things could be worse. My parents could have been poor. We might have had nothing to eat. We could have been living on welfare. Or worse, someone in my family, or even I, could have a horrible disease. That would be unbearable!"

Kate wishes she could change her life with the snap of a finger. She imagines life could be better if she hung out with people who smile and don't have as many issues as she has. She wonders if being with people who have courage could help her live a better life. She thinks if she moves out of town, things may change for her. Perhaps she could find a better job, and/or travel and see new things. These thoughts help Kate understand her situation. She begins to think running away would be a path to survival and that only then, things might get better.

Comments on situation 2:

When you exist with negativity, you may invite undesirable issues that become entangled, like a cobweb, with your existence. You are caught in a dead-end situation. Just by wishing. you cannot have a better life. If you want to be like those who seem to be alive and happy, you have to change.

It can be challenging to develop the habit of moving forward in a healthy manner, but it is both possible and worthwhile. You cannot make progress by just moving from one place to another, or mingling with people who are "happy campers." As the saying goes, birds of a feather flock together – happy campers tend to associate with other happy campers.

Negativity comes from within and is deep set. It is like a whirl-pool, going around and around, without purpose. You just exist and make do. A positive attitude is vital if you are to change, and welcome a smile and the good feelings that come with it. When you experience the richness of living with positivity, you won't turn away from it. You can just hop on the wagon and head to your destination, enjoying positive energy. Life can be beautiful! You are responsible for the effects of a happy heart, which result in smiles and a desire for more!

Situation 3 (The unsatisfied, "Why me?" attitude)

Let's look at an example of a someone who has an unsatisfied, "Why me?" attitude and does not experience the simple freedom of being who he is – the freedom to be.

> *Miles seemed to be growing in the right direction but he has experienced a down-turn. He feels frustrated, perplexed and has anxiety attacks.*
>
> *Miles had a good upbringing. His parents were attentive to his needs and comfort, both mentally and physically.*
>
> *Yet Miles felt something wasn't quite right. He couldn't put his finger on it, in spite of the fact that his growing-up years were decent. He lacks confidence and is afraid of making mistakes.*
>
> *Miles went to university but he missed out on a lot while he was there. He wasn't very interested in school or indeed, in life, in general. He was just going through the motions.*

Miles is neither an extrovert nor an introvert. He has friends but rather than initiating activities, he just goes with the flow. He finds that nothing is exciting, and he has no dreams or goals. He doesn't look forward to each new day, even though he doesn't seem to be depressed. He just lives through each day, in a humdrum, routine kind of way.

Perhaps because of the support Miles had at home, he has some leeway in figuring out what's going on in his mind and emotions. He feels he has to get to the bottom of this in order to feel better and appreciate his life, as others seem to appreciate theirs.

Miles observes others who are ambitious and happy, moving forward in anticipation of life events, and living in peace. He wants the same happy feeling he had as a youngster – for example, the way he felt when he learned to ride a bike. If he fell off his bike, he would get up and try again until he succeeded. He yearned for exciting experiences – that was what drove him forward in life. Back then, he had positive energy. Now, he wants that same feeling – a love of life, with no qualms about living.

But during and after university, Miles lost his zest for life. As time went on, his life became mundane and depressing. He needs to determine why he feels this way. He needs to break free of this humdrum, dull existence, in which he has little ambition, no energy, and sometimes, even thinks of finding a way out.

Comments on situation 3

The results are similar in any situation where there is negativity. Along with a lack of energy, other issues may pop up. Even though you have a decent family, you may have undesirable feelings. Why? A major reason is a lack of confidence, which affects your journey through life.

You may try too hard and feel you never achieve excellence. It's not easy being a perfectionist. More important, it's painful and it leaves no room for you to grow, as a person. It actually prevents you from achieving your goals, and it has negative side-effects, such as anguish, anxiety and headaches.

You must realize it is okay to be imperfect. After all, <u>no one is perfect</u>, even the perfectionist! When you learn how to ride a bike, it's challenging, but you do it. When you don't get all the right answers at school, it's okay. Your lack of interest in school may be because you find it a drag to live with a results-focused attitude.

Trying to be perfect uses up energy, and so, you already feel let down, negative and discouraged – without even realizing it. This doesn't help you fulfill your dreams and goals! You must accept life's situations and then move on. You must be open to the fact that we do not live in a perfect world. Through practice, by embracing the positive, avoiding the negative, and living on the positive side of the pole, you can be happy, no matter what happens!

Prepare for a change from negativity to positivity. By living life in this way, you will develop good habits, win the battle of entanglement and achieve total freedom!

Situation 4 (Controlling your environment – The freedom "to be" is not in sight!)

Let's look at an example of a someone who was born into a life where she was nourished with inner resources, gained through various experiences, such as learning by making mistakes and using them as fuel for healthy living.

> *Louise's mother tended to decide her every move, and Louise was used to this. Her mother oversaw everything her daughter did, even selecting the clothes Louise would wear. Louise tended to stay close to home. At age 11, she was a very*

responsible child. She did various chores, such as babysitting her younger brother, but she had no life of her own. She took her marching orders from her mother – this felt normal to her. So, it's not surprising she had a negative attitude!

To avoid arguments, Louise listened to her mother. She felt she could never win, anyway. Louise's mother would make phone calls for her, and rarely let her daughter out of her sight.

Louise felt both of her parents loved her. Her mother seemed to be in charge of how the household should run which included raising her children supervising different activities in school and the like.

Louise went off to school, and had very good marks. Later, she focused on teaching English as a second language, which she loved.

While growing up, Louise missed out on many opportunities. She knew she was missing out, and she found this very painful. It made her feel sad because she had not been allowed to explore life and engage in the kind of activities her friends were involved in.

Later, Louise met a man, began a relationship with him and moved far from her childhood home. But Louise's partner was very controlling. That was all she had known; it had been the pattern of her life. Like Louise's mother, he meant well, and as he often said to her, he loved her deeply.

However, this new relationship placed Louise in a situation that was worse than in her childhood home. She was an adult, but she still lived as if she were in her childhood prison. Her partner never harmed her physically, but he was emotionally abusive. He behaved as if he was her boss.

Louise loved her work as a teacher. She also loved to cook and go to the gym. But just as she had kept things from her mother, she also kept things from her partner. She felt she never knew who she really was. Once again, this made her feel sad.

But Louise put a smile on her face to cover up her true feelings. The expression, "Put on a happy face!" summed up how she presented her outer self to the world. How she felt on the inside was another story.

Louise taught English to francophone students. She was completely immersed in her Teaching and was well respected at work. Her students thought she was awesome. As a Result, she had a window into a life of freedom

!But the strain of constantly covering up her true self eventually caught up with Louise. She developed headaches, and pain in her back and legs. In fact, all the negativity within her seemed to poison her body. She took medication for anxiety. She never talked to her partner about the true state of her feelings. Instead, she swept everything under the rug.

Later, Louise experienced some serious health issues. It took a year to recover, much of which she spent in hospital. But finally, Louise came home and gradually grew stronger. However, she still felt stuck, with no sense of freedom – that familiar feeling of living in a prison remained.

Louise is no longer able to teach. When she sees her doctor, her partner always accompanies her, so she cannot share her inner concerns with her physician.

At one point, Louise wants to run away but she stays, and the rest is history, as they say. Her partner is kind to her, but he is oblivious to his own controlling nature. However, he is good at organizing activities, such as dinners at the best restaurants, exciting trips, etc. Louise and her partner enjoy travelling together. They have visited Canada's North, exploring Nunavik, the most northerly part of Quebec, where they met Inuit people, and enjoyed learning about their culture and traditions. They have also travelled to other regions of the world, including Russia and the Middle East.

At last, Louise's partner asks her to marry him. He had been wanting to marry her since they first got together, but she had not been interested. But she finally gives in. After her long illness, it seems that she no longer asserts herself.

Louise still lives with negativity. She is a very bright woman, with so much to offer. But her negativity has prevented from expressing her true self – a very sad reality.

Comments on situation 4

Louise's mother loved her. But she did not give her daughter the chance to grow, and to experience life fully. She did not allow Louise to be independent and gain the knowledge that would allow her to live a full life, and learn through her own mistakes.

Some parents block their children's path to a full life and to learn from experience. This prevents them from tackling the life challenges they must face in order to grow and become independent, to gain a sense of themselves, and to grow strong, confident and happy, while achieving their goals.

A child who is learning to walk may fall many times before they succeed in walking on their own. The same applies to a person who is learning how to cope with life's ups and downs. It is vitally important that a child experience life fully. It is hard for a parent to witness how painful that may be for their child. To grow, a child must experience and learn, each step of the way. It is like using a map on a clear day; the parents may be the clouds that prevent the child's growth, which takes place through a process of falling and getting up again.

The child must be able live through a process of trial and error, finally gaining the insights they need to move beyond the challenges, and reap the rewards of achievement. That is a life of positivity, and it is the key to living every day as it comes, with inward strength and resilience.

Conclusion

The above situations are just a few examples of people who live a life of negativity, without realizing that positive change can make a world of difference for them. Everyone has the right to live with inner peace, and to love life! Living a negative life is simply a habit. With practice, anyone can change their life, and make it completely different. It takes strength and will to change and surround oneself with positive people who smile, are excited about life and achieve their goals.

Instead of just wishing to be positive, you can <u>be</u> positive. You can achieve this if you persevere, and work toward the goal of enjoying each day as it comes, tackling different situations without anguish. Live with the energy you need to get through the life's challenges. It is an experience in which we can <u>all</u> share.

There is no excuse for simply existing instead of living. Whether you have been abused, lived in poverty, or had your heart broken, you still can find the way forward.

For example, an alcoholic who hits rock bottom is capable of living a different life. <u>There is a way out</u>, and that is by changing, doing what you need to do, and living on the positive side of the pole. Once you are on that side, there is no going back. You have tasted the difference between living instead of just existing.

If you persist, you will get there. You must ease your way toward the positive feeling. You must let go of the past, no matter what you endured. Your life can change. You can be in charge of yourself if you use the "Tools" described in the next chapter.

CHAPTER 4

(Prepare) and use Tools

To change from a negative attitude to a positive attitude, you need some tools to help you live on the positive side of the pole and attain success.

Preparing for your adventure –to begin living instead of just existing – calls for a plan that includes **preparation**, **motivation** and **commitment**. You must follow this plan and never give up, under any circumstances. Before **kickoff** – that moment when you launch your adventure – you must concentrate on the tools at hand and focus on using them diligently.

As you move forward, your inner energy will begin to grow, giving you a feeling of being in control. Your reward is an enriched life. The change you'll experience within yourself will become your new normal, bringing you zest for living.

Preparation

Preparation is key to creating a new way of life, in which you will gain confidence, energy and a healthy lifestyle. And all of this comes only if you persevere, with an "I-will-win" attitude!

If you are to achieve your goals, you must recognize that preparation takes time, especially if the challenge ahead demands courage. It takes time for you to acknowledge the positive changes within yourself as you move toward the positive side of the pole. You must embrace this as a vivid state of being, coupled with the determination you need to fulfill the task ahead.

You must also practice a new way of thinking, using words that reflect your positive attitude. For example, you must think, "I want a complete change – a positive change that will help me build energy. I am excited, and I can't wait to live with a smile, with positive energy, and the ability to achieve good results every day." You must not allow yourself to engage in any negative thinking!

Preparation helps you to persevere and stay focused on your goal. First and foremost, you must make the commitment to never give up! When you complete your preparation, remaining motivated and committed, you will be better equipped to tackle the section on "Tools."

However, you'll need patience. While this is no easy task, it is attainable. It's difficult to change a habit and therein lies the challenge. If you're prepared and never willing to give up, you'll be starting from a good, strong place.

For example, when you have prepared well for an exam at school, and you achieve success, it's thanks to your good planning. You must prepare well. Your confidence will be your strength!

After you complete your **Preparation** exercise and you feel confident, you can move on to the next step, which is **motivation**.

Motivation

Motivation leads to positive feelings. It strengthens your will to move forward. When you're motivated, you're on the right track. No one can stop you or discourage you. You're in charge and no one can stop your growth. As you move toward your goals, you can conquer and crush the negatives. This is what being positive means. Motivation must be present before you can move on to using the **Tools**. By then, you will understand this truth: "Where there's a will, there's a way."

Commitment

After going through the **Preparation** and **Motivation** exercises, you won't find **Commitment** to be a big challenge. When you feel strong about commitment, it's another feather in your cap. You can move along without worries, discouragement or negative thoughts. You are ready to grow and achieve!

Growing is like building a house – you must start with a solid foundation. This allows you to continue to the next level. Whether you're building the main floor with its various rooms, or installing window frames; your work never stops. You remain committed until the house is finished.

When you're committed, nothing will stop you from reaching the positive side of the pole. You will find that continued growth and meeting your goals give you a sense of achievement. You'll never want to return to the negative side because you have experienced what a good life feels like, and you feel invigorated!

Preparation, **Motivation** and **Commitment** are prerequisites to what I call the **Powerhouse**. These are the **Tools** that keep you on track, living with positivity – a habit that you'll develop with practice. You have built the framework through **preparation**, **motivation** and **commitment** – the three necessary elements of the blueprint that gives you confidence, strength, and determination to move to the next level. The blueprint guides you toward a practice that gives you a framework. This helps determine your direction in pursuing your new way of life – a life full of rewards that keep you on the right track, wanting more energy and success.

You must use the **Tools** appropriately to get the job done! **Tools** keep you on the right track, getting you to the positive side and helping you stay there! As a result, you must engrave them on your mind. They are your tools to use over and over again. Eventually, these tools will feel normal to you, and you will use them with comfort and ease, allowing energy to grow, day by day!

Now that you have done the ground work, through **preparation**, **motivation** and **commitment**, as well as the use of the **tools**, you're ready for the challenge! When you're ready, you're a winner in the making – a star achiever, who excels at any activity you choose, whether it's swimming, running, show jumping, acting, etc.

We all have opportunities, choices and dreams. Some people, however, just don't believe in themselves. Those who desire a very good life can be highly successful and able to persevere. What is exciting is that once you achieve that good feeling and gain the desire for more, your reward will be inner happiness. You'll be ready to tackle any challenge that comes your way, without deep anxiety and pain.

Your journey to the positive side of the pole will give you enough joy and satisfaction to last your whole life through.

Tools

Tool 1 – Never wake up with a negative feeling, thought or comment. Open your eyes, and instantly, begin your day with a positive thought. For example, if it's snowing, know that while you'll have to shovel snow, it's good exercise and you'll feel great after it's done.

In this way, starting off on the right foot every day will become a habit, giving you the energy you need to experience a positive attitude, allowing you to generate new ideas, and new goals – a strategy that becomes the new norm and a way to succeed in every project you undertake. Why? Because you're in control, on the positive side of the pole. Thanks to your efforts, you can take on anything without being crushed.

Tool 2

Tool 2 is a prerequisite of Tool 1

Make it a practice to repeat Tool 1 every day, when you wake up. Practice it until it becomes second nature. In other words, once it feels natural to launch each day on a positive note, it is a mark of true achievement. Through repetition, a daily practice becomes a habit!

Don't cut corners, or put it off until the next day, thinking, "I'll do better tomorrow." It is vital to achieve a positive attitude each day, from the moment you wake up. It's evidence that you're on the right track, not thinking of your progress as mere practice but rather as your new way of life. You'll be living on the positive side of the pole, effortlessly, simply moving along to the next step.

You'll discover that your negative thoughts will begin to fade away. The practice of thinking positive thoughts each day, all day, is exactly what you want. There's no going back. You have established a good habit that becomes a part of your life, helping you feel great, and achieve your goals. You're in the driver's seat, in charge and loving every minute. With your armour of positivity in place, you have a good defence that will never fail you because you are strong and living a life that is full of joy.

Tool 3 – Leave no stone unturned

To achieve a level of positivity that is free of anxiety, you must be vigilant, leaving no stone unturned. Make it a way of life to establish a practice of living on the positive side of the pole. Being vigilant simply means being aware and wanting more of the good feelings, every day. You're already in charge because, as the expression goes, practice makes perfect!

For example, for an athlete, being in charge means regular practice, while remaining aware of one's goals and achievements. Because you practice and enjoy your positive thoughts, growth and success are inevitable. In other words, you reap what you sow! This mental activity becomes second nature to you. You have no negative thoughts and you don't feel as if you <u>have</u> to do this. It is your choice to do it! You will be energized, enjoying each day and each year that lies ahead.

You are in good condition, both physically and mentally, which in turn, ensures your continued progress. Feeling creative, feeling good about yourself and loving life all become natural. In other words, you will be attracted to those who are similar to you, and that's exactly what you should expect. You will fit in, and find your own turf, so to speak – a familiar area among those who, like you, have discovered the experience of quality living.

CHAPTER 5

The Challenges Facing Students

For college or university students, life can feel like a roller coaster. The challenges may seem unbearable. Students may feel they're lost in a sea of negative existence, with no room for growth or gratification. They may feel entangled and trapped, going around in a too-familiar pattern. They may find their studies confusing, which in turn, affects their personal lives.

Students may wonder, "What's going on? Every day, it's the 'same-old, same-old!'" Existing like this is counter-productive. Students may be unable to shake off that feeling. Is there another option? Yes! So, let's transform and perform!

First, it's important to remember that when you live with negativity, you can develop mental and physical anguish. Bad feelings and uneasiness complicate your situation, and may lead you to making rash decisions. This prevents you from having good feelings, which are key to developing a positive attitude.

Perhaps it sounds ironic, but another factor in helping you to invite success into your life is to face pain. As much as pain is an uncomfortable part of your life, facing it is important if you are to move on. You must set goals and note your accomplishments. Such forward-thinking, positive actions are vital to your plan for success. Directing your path in life and finding ways to change the status quo strengthen your ability to look forward to each day.

For many students, living with negativity leads to a very uncomfortable existence. You may find yourself just plodding along, feeling exhausted. You may try to cope with unpleasant feelings and the associated ailments, including anxiety, headaches, stress, sleeplessness, to name just a few. All this can feel excruciating.

Existing like this inhibits your productivity, no matter how much effort you put into trying to have a positive attitude. Living like this is indeed difficult. But it doesn't have to be like this – you must be willing to change!

It can be tempting to make rash decisions. Making quick decisions may feel like you've gained a much-needed breather. Students may try to "change the landscape," to alter their feeling that life is almost unbearable. They think a change from the old pattern sounds all right; they may welcome the chance to just have a good time. So, off to the bars and parties they go, to indulge in beer and booze, cannabis and camaraderie, discovering they and their counterparts all share the same woes – that "everything sucks," no matter what.

Parents, siblings and old friends just don't seem to get it. The "highs" feel so welcome. Those who are on the same wavelength seem to understand and listen. Yes, it's that old scenario – "misery loves company." Many students just accept the downside of those college years, and continue living in turmoil. Students don't get caught up in just one kind of existence, as in, Hamlet's "To be or not to be…" Depressing thoughts may arise in different scenarios, even making you feel that death is better than living. Those thoughts may result from a habit of sad living – that is, choosing negativity.

Feeling overwhelmed and distraught can be discouraging. But there is a way out – a way you can change your path in life. When you feel as if you have reached rock bottom, the old adage to "pull yourself up by your own bootstraps" can help you move toward a success – a success achieved through your own efforts. In other words, a positive move is in the works!

To start off on good footing, you must address your issues, one by one, paying particular attention to your every-day habits. This is a prerequisite – you must do this before embarking on your journey to success. This allows you to see how you begin your day. And more important, it allows you to compare your journey to others who reach their goals. You can then identify and avoid the drawbacks you and others may have encountered.

Before you can compare your journey with that of others, there are a few things you must do first.

On a notepad, write down the details of your daily life on the left-hand side of the page. Include information from the moment you wake up in the morning to when you go to bed at night. It is important that you note everything you do, whether it's having your morning coffee, rushing to leave home for school, forgetting this or that, tripping over your favorite boots. Whatever it may be, make a note of every activity, including any negative comments you may have.

On the right-hand side of the page, make notes about starting a new life. Review chapter four, the "Tools" section of this book, and begin to go through every activity. But this time, note your positive comments. For example, do not allow even one thought that is negative. With a positive attitude, you must record every action you carry out. no matter what the activity. For example, you arrive at school, your notepad in hand, you take notes during class, you never miss a class, and so on. To accomplish all this, you must get to bed at a decent time – for some of us, this might be a huge change! But you must do it – no excuses allowed!

This is a clean-slate approach, as you move toward a healthier way of life. It takes practice; it's not easy but it is possible. Your reward is that you will gain energy, with no negativity. Eventually, this new way of life will become second nature. You can breathe easier, feel calmer if you practice every day, without ceasing, until you feel a change. That's when the good life begins.

Before you can move forward, you must face the pain that brought you to the negative side of your life, in which unpleasant feelings persist. In a sense, you must face the music, feel how you feel today. You must focus on and absorb your life – a life of pain – without running away from the reality of the moment.

Right now you may not be a happy camper. If so, concentrate on your daily way of living. Perhaps you're just going through the motions, feeling trapped. You must address the negative thoughts that arise in your heart and mind. This kind of all-encompassing, low-grade feeling is similar to mourning - the kind of pain you feel for a dying or deceased loved one. Facing the pain will help you heal. Running away or passing over the pain will prevent you from moving on to life's better side.

Once you have absorbed and understood your feelings, you can really get into the nitty-gritty of it all – for example, discovering why you're not sleeping well, why you have headaches, and why you lose valuable time trying, but failing, to do the right thing. After all, you can't move on until you change the way you think and regain your lost energy. It's like trying to run a marathon without prior training and practice – you lack commitment and simply don't feel up to it. To carry on like this, retaining the pain and related problems, is a complete waste of time and effort!

Once you have experienced and paid attention to your pain and sad thoughts, you can move on to the next step – a clean slate, a new way of life, a breather. You will find this encouraging because it allows you the space you need to grow and breathe. It allows the good thoughts and feelings to emerge. You will feel a new beginning stirring in the air. There will be no more sleepless nights and no more headaches. You will feel more serious about tackling your daily challenges. You will accomplish your goals and no longer feel compelled to make rash decisions.

As you will discover, all of this will be a huge change for you! Now, you are working on yourself, doing what is good for your growth and happiness. You will be able to plan your days, and take care of your daily tasks and commitments You will feel energized and ready to meet the next day's challenges and opportunities.

So, what happens now? You are living with positive, healthy thoughts, but what does that mean? It means your energy level is increasing, and you are able to leave negative thoughts behind, bit by bit. This takes practice, however, because your habit has been negativity. It is still alive and well, inside you – <u>but</u>, it's on the way out!

Practice is the only way to make it to the other side of the pole – the positive side. When you feel you are well-positioned to move on, you will also feel that the end of negativity is close. Soon, you will no longer feel trapped, not knowing how to find your way out of the woods. You must go through each step to discover a new way of life. Greater endurance will strengthen you, and help you find your chosen path in life, where you will feel free, at last!

Determining your goals and accomplishing them will change your whole way of life. You need a plan to identify and reach for your goals. It's like building a house from scratch – you need a blueprint that lays out your plan. You must organize your thoughts and resources – for example, what materials and tools do you need? You must ensure there are no negatives as you go along – and negatives include thoughts like these: "I can't do this; it's too hot; I don't know where to start." And the list goes on.

You must not allow negativity into the equation at any time. You are changing, building a new life, finding a new direction. Along the way, you will take steps toward healthy growth. So, you need to make a true transformation – indeed, an evolution – to realize your new beginning, in which you will focus on your new life.

For example, you'll need to clearly envision how you will feel in your new home. That means clearing your mind, leaving no cobwebs behind. Clarity and the ability to move on are positive; they indicate you're on the right track. That's why earlier, I gave the example of a well-constructed home. It's based on a blueprint – a clear, solid plan – and it's built with good materials, tools and techniques. This example also applies to your life as a student. Each day, you organize your schedule to ensure it runs smoothly, one step at a time. Just as you would not skip a chapter in your readings prior to your exam, you build a house one board at a time, one nail at a time, according to the plan.

You must also consider your personal traits. We humans possess particular traits we express through our characters, which are all different. For example, your aim is to develop the positive attitude you need to overcome a negative way of being. You may wonder, "Why does another person who has lived with negativity made it to the other side of the pole with less difficulty than I?"

In part, it could be because of the traits we possess. These traits lead us to react in a particular way that might not be conducive to a smooth transition toward a positive attitude. For example, if someone is impatient and nervous, they may have a tendency to become agitated and frustrated. For such people, it's a good idea to for them to stop trying to move on when they feel impatient or agitated, then pause and return to where they left off. We must be aware of our inner traits and work on how best to proceed to get the result we want. The result – we can be ready to get into gear and move on.

Aside from each of us being a unique individual, born with different traits, we all have had a different upbringing – even siblings raised in the same family. Our differing traits indicate how different we all are from each other. You can choose to change, no matter what kind of upbringing you experienced. This, in itself, becomes enticing, for you can cultivate your own garden as it is embedded in your own brain. A fresh start can mean you can experience healthy growth, a feeling of strength, and a determination to live well. Adjusting to a different way of life – a life worth living in which you enjoy each day as it comes – is a choice and therefore can be achieved

Imagine a beautiful orchard, where the scent of fruit trees makes your mouth water. Or imagine a vegetable garden exploding with new growth and many different colours. Imagine simply feeling great – a feeling that grows from inside you. Yes, a well-kept garden is within you; it is the result of healthy growth.

When you engage in the process of building a home, you often have to work around some tough areas. You may have to remove huge stones or debris, or deal with other unwanted surprises. These obstacles can all be very challenging; they can cause frustrating delays in the progress of building your home. Physical work has its obstacles and its nuisances – in fact, the two often go hand in hand.

But the feeling of being in charge is powerful. Somehow, you find ways to get through the challenges of the hard, physical work. You also discover ways to bring to fruition your carefully thought-out ideas. It all becomes something you can tackle, work through and achieve.

But you need the good that comes from feeling confident if you are to work to create positive and lasting change from within yourself. By sticking to your plan, you'll have concrete results and that winning feeling of success, thanks to your well-earned accomplishments!

Achieving your goals is the icing on the cake. It provides you with a huge boost, a positive feeling, and it moves you toward a feeling of contentment within yourself and with your situation. Your practice of bringing a positive attitude to each new day becomes second nature. Fulfilling your goals is your reward – in a sense, it is the compensation for not giving up. Your ambition has been to gain the energy you need to change your life, to make it a good life – not just for now, but forever. Now, you can consider it a *fait accompli*!

On another note, it's important to keep in mind that everyone has faults, failings and weaknesses. For example, some people are easily stumped, unable to move forward if they feel a project isn't going well enough. These people are often perfectionists. They may waste a lot of time trying to attain perfection, which is not only a nuisance, but also, impossible. Nothing can be perfect. This behaviour prevents people from moving on – or worse, it may make them want to give up. It's not easy to change this kind of mindset, but with practice, it can be done. In my opinion, overdoing a project that is already being done well is a kind of compulsive behavior, much like feeling compelled to put your foot on every crack when you walk on the sidewalk!

We must take ownership of our own foibles. But there are many roadblocks we must rearrange if we are to acknowledge our weaknesses – and we must do this if we are to move forward. Failing to take ownership of our limitations can inhibit our ability to progress. Procrastinators – the stallers among us – may wait and wait before making a move. It may simply be in their nature to delay like this. There are many reasons people procrastinate – for example, they may be fearful of trying at all, in case they don't succeed – in other words, a fear of failure; they may find that trying is too much of a hassle; they may feel overwhelmed – and the list goes on.

We often hear that misery loves company, and that is not entirely a bad thing. Knowing we are not alone in feeling miserable allows us to absorb and understand the fact that people are people, and that we all have our idiosyncrasies.

But remember: perfection does not exist! Making mistakes is a key way for us to learn, grow and benefit from our mistakes. Doing the work to fulfill our goals is a key factor in achieving success. Where there's a will, there's a way!

I strongly recommend that you keep and use the tools you encountered in chapter four, at all times. Keeping your tools close at hand keeps you on the right path and moving on. You need all the pieces of the puzzle to keep your thoughts positive, without distraction and the risk of frustration. This the key to moving on, without irritation. That ensures a smooth ride, as much as possible!

Also keep in mind that as students, you are in charge of your own lives. It should encourage you to know you have the skills, know-how and determination get out of whatever mess you're in. You have what it takes to make a change, and to be free and feel comfortable in your life. Then you will have the space to breathe and cherish the change that you have chosen for your life.

In the process, you will find the roller coaster of life will feel like less of a challenge, and you'll be able to accept it more easily. This is because you're in charge. You are in touch with your inner strength. This awareness eases whatever unexpected surprises you may encounter. The unexpected can invade your life like a rain storm invades your own well- nourished garden. It may be unpleasant in the moment, but it has it benefits, in the long term.

When you take the hits or the negativities that come along, you can easily push them away, thanks to your built-in armor – which <u>you</u> created yourself, through the invaluable choice you made to live, as opposed to simply existing!

You feel strong and in charge of your life because you:

• followed the steps, day by day out;
• worked on issues to change your position from negative to positive; and
• did your best to reach your goal.

You have chosen to win, and to never stop in your mission until you truly feel you have made it, and there's no going back.

Practice makes perfect – it's the proof of the pudding! You made it because of your tenacity, and your eagle-eye on the goal of positive change, which has now become second nature.

Good feelings within take over your life and you will become productive, reaching a comfort zone beyond your imagination. Your wakeup call has served you well, giving you a light at the end of the tunnel – a light you can see and toward which you can move!

Being tuned into your new way of living gives you the green light to move forward. It gives you a broader outlook on your choices and dreams, and the knowledge and energy to fulfill them. Now, you are mentally ready to advance because you understand how simple life can be. You are free to simply be within your life. You no longer have unwelcome thoughts that can drain our energy, and put proverbial sticks in your bicycle wheels, stopping you from move forward smoothly.

There is a reward for sticking to the plan of maintaining a positive attitude. By choosing to live well, you will change your life in a very positive way. You will accomplish much – and not only for yourself. Remember, birds of a feather flock together. Whether it's your partner or partner-to-be, your children, your friends, the people you choose to have in your life will generally be healthy, like you, reflecting your own joie de vivre.

You have your guide in chapter four, which lays out the tools you need. Keep them with you at all times! Your choices in life are yours to make. Everyone can succeed. Diligence and practice will give you the "Yes I can!" attitude. Once you feel strength and confidence grow within you, there is no turning back. You are in charge.

Remember, living with good energy is the key – it's like magic, except it's not actually magic. It's the result of your own diligent work, keeping at it, day in day out, never giving up. That is how you succeed.

Printed in the United States
By Bookmasters